soul honey

michael mosesian

Soul Honey: Poems on Self-Love, Healing & Self-Discovery

Publisher: Absolute Author Publishing House

Library of Congress In-Publication Data
Mosesian, Michael

ISBN: 979-8-89401-067-0

Editing services by Melanie Underwood
Book illustrations by Fatima Seehar
Cover illustrations by Katarina Naskovski

Contents

Embracing the Present

The Moment of Choice

The world throws its stones,
words that sting,
events that hurt,
and your body remembers the ancient way:
to flinch, to fight, to flee.

This is reaction, a reflex born in the primal past.

But between the trigger and the action
lies a breath,
a space,
a moment of choice.

This is where you reclaim your power.

This is where you learn to respond.

Not with the knee-jerk of fear,
but with the wisdom of awareness.

The breath is the bridge
between the wild horse of impulse
and the steady hand of intention.

Choose the breath.
Choose the response.
Choose the path that leads to your highest self.

The Unwatered Garden

Do not be a gardener who only waters the roses,
ignoring the weeds,
the parched earth,
the plants that need shade.

Your soul is a garden too,
and it requires tending in all its parts,
not just the bright and blossoming ones.

Joy is beautiful,
but sorrow needs your attention too.
Happiness is a gift,
but anger has something to teach you.

Do not be afraid of the shadows in your garden.
They are not invaders,
but inhabitants that need your care.
Acknowledge them.
Learn from them.

Only then will your garden truly flourish,
in all its wild,
untamed,
authentic beauty.

Tending the Spring

You are not a stagnant pool,
but a spring,
a source of energy that flows in cycles.
Do not apologize for the times you need to be still,
to gather strength for the next surge.

The world will demand and demand,
but you are not obligated to give
every last drop.

Your energy is precious,
a sacred resource to be guarded,
cherished, and used wisely.

Learn to say "no,"
not as a rejection,
but as an act of self-preservation.

Honor your need for rest,
for solitude,
for quiet.

The spring within needs tending.
Only then can it surge again
with life,
with creativity,
with love.

The Illusion of Control

We try to control time,
to manage it,
to schedule it,
to make it fit our plans.

But time is a slippery thing,
it eludes our grasp,
it defies our attempts to contain it.

We are not the masters of time,
but its passengers,
carried along by its relentless flow.

The more we try to control it,
the more we suffer,
the more we feel its passage as a burden.

Let go of the illusion of control.
Embrace the uncertainty.
Surrender to the rhythm of time.

In that surrender,
you will find freedom,
peace, and a deeper appreciation
for the preciousness of each moment.

The Invitation

This is an invitation to come home to yourself.
To shed the layers of who you think you should be.
To embrace the wholeness of who you are.

It is an invitation to listen to the whispers of your heart.
To follow the compass of your intuition.
To dance to the rhythm of your soul.

It's an invitation to forgive yourself for the past.
To love yourself in the present.
To believe in the beauty of your future.

This journey will not be easy.
There will be challenges and setbacks.
But it will be worth it.

Because on the other side of fear, doubt, and pain.
Lies a freedom, a joy, a peace that you have never known.

So, take a deep breath.
And begin.
Your journey home awaits.

The Eternal Now

Beyond the tick-tock of the clock,
beyond the turning of the calendar pages,
lies the eternal now,
the still point in the turning world.

It is the present moment,
fully embraced,
without judgment,
without resistance.

It is where past and future dissolve,
and only the immediacy of experience remains.

In the eternal now,
there is no time,
only being.

It is a state of grace,
a glimpse into the timeless nature of reality.
Seek the eternal now.
It is always available,
hidden in plain sight,
waiting to be discovered within the present moment.

The Clock of the Heart

Your heart has its own clock,
a rhythm that does not always align
with the ticking of the world.

It may beat faster in moments of fear or excitement,
slower in times of peace or sorrow.
It may skip a beat altogether when you are surprised
by love or joy.

Do not try to force your heart to conform
to the rigid schedule of external time.
Honor its unique tempo.

Healing takes time,
growth takes time,
self-discovery takes time.

Listen to the clock of your heart.
It knows the pace that is right for you.
It will guide you toward a life
that is lived in harmony with your deepest self.

Savor Each Moment

Simply to be alive is a gift,
a miracle,
an opportunity to experience the wonder
and the beauty of existence.

To breathe,
to feel,
to think,
to love,
to connect,
to create,
to learn,
to grow.

These are the gifts of being human.
Do not take them for granted.

Savor each moment.
Appreciate the simple pleasures.
Express your gratitude for the life you have been given.

Life is not always easy.
It can be challenging,
painful,
and unpredictable.

But it is also precious,
extraordinary,
and filled with infinite possibilities.

Embrace the gift of being.
Live your life fully,
authentically,
and with an open heart.

The Ripple Effect of Gratitude

Gratitude is a powerful force,
a transformative energy that shifts your perspective,
opens your heart,
and connects you to the abundance of life.

It is the practice of noticing and appreciating
the good things,
both big and small,
that are already present in your experience.

Gratitude is not about ignoring the challenges
or denying the pain.
It is about choosing to focus on what is working,
what is beautiful,
what is worthy of appreciation,
even in the midst of difficulty.

Cultivate a daily practice of gratitude.
Express your appreciation to others.
Take time to savor the simple pleasures.

The more you practice gratitude, the more
you will find to be grateful for.
It is a key that unlocks joy,
resilience, and a deeper connection to life.

The Illusion of Lost Time

You may feel that you have lost time,
wasted it on the wrong paths,
the wrong people,
the wrong pursuits.

But time is never truly lost.
It is transformed.
It becomes experience,
wisdom,
lessons learned.

Even the detours,
the stumbles,
the seemingly wasted moments,
have contributed to who you are today.

Do not dwell in regret.
Do not berate yourself for the past.
Instead, glean the wisdom from those experiences.

Use them as fuel for growth,
as stepping stones toward a brighter future.

Time is not linear.
It is a flowing river, ever-changing.
And even when you feel lost,
you are always moving forward.
You are always learning.

The Joy of Noticing

The world is full of wonders,
waiting to be noticed,
waiting to be appreciated.
The smallest details hold immense beauty.

The intricate pattern of a leaf,
the way the sunlight dapples through the trees,
the cool, smooth surface of a river stone,
the kindness in a stranger's smile,
the sound of rain on a windowpane,
the earthy scent of petrichor rising from the ground,
the sweet taste of a ripe berry plucked from the bush.

Train yourself to notice.
Cultivate a sense of wonder.
Experience the world with all your senses,
as if for the first time.

Joy is not found in grand events,
but in the accumulation of small moments of noticing,
of appreciating,
of being fully present to the beauty that surrounds you.

Open your senses.
Open your heart.
The world is waiting to amaze you, every single moment.

The Gift of the Present Moment

The past is gone.
The future is yet to come.
All you truly have is this present moment.

Do not let it slip away unnoticed,
unappreciated.

Be here now.
Fully present in your life.

Savor the small joys.
Feel the warmth of the sun on your skin.
Listen to the laughter of loved ones.
Taste the sweetness of a ripe fruit.

This moment is a gift.
That is why it is called the present.

Do not waste it worrying about the future
or regretting the past.

Embrace the present moment.
It is the only place where life truly happens.
It is where you can make a difference,
in your life and others'.
It is the only time you can choose to change your life.

The Thief of Time

Regret is a thief of time,
stealing the joy of the present moment
by dwelling on the unchangeable past.

Worry is a thief of time,
robbing you of peace
by anticipating a future that may never come.

Procrastination is a thief of time,
delaying action,
postponing dreams,
allowing precious moments to slip away.

Do not let these thieves steal your time.
Be mindful of their presence.
Choose to focus on what you can control:
your actions,
your thoughts,
your attitude in the present moment.

Your time is your most valuable asset.
Spend it wisely.
Spend it consciously.
Spend it on what truly matters.

The Kindness of Strangers

A smile from a passerby,
a door held open,
a helping hand offered.
Small acts of kindness from strangers,
unexpected and heartwarming.

They are reminders that we are all connected,
that compassion exists,
even in the midst of a busy world.

These small moments can brighten our day,
restore our faith in humanity,
and inspire us to pay it forward.

Be open to the kindness of strangers.
And be a source of kindness yourself.
You never know how much a small gesture
can mean to someone.

The Rearview Mirror

The past is like a rearview mirror,
offering a glimpse of where we have been,
but not a map of where we are going.

We can glance at it,
learn from it,
but we cannot drive our lives looking backward.

The road ahead is uncharted,
full of possibilities,
waiting for us to create our own path.

Use the rearview mirror wisely.
Acknowledge the lessons of the past,
but keep your eyes focused on the present,
and your heart open to the future.

Courage
and Resilience

The Bravery of Being Seen

To be truly seen,
flaws and all,
and still be loved,
is perhaps the greatest bravery of all.

It is shedding the masks,
dropping the pretense,
and daring to stand vulnerable
before another.

It is risking rejection,
judgment, misunderstanding,
in the hope of finding connection,
acceptance, belonging.

It is saying, "This is me,
all of me,
the light and the shadow,
the beauty and the chaos."

It is a leap of faith,
a tremulous step into the unknown.
But in that vulnerability,
there is a profound strength.

To be seen and loved
for who you truly are
is to know you are worthy,
you are enough.
It is freedom.

The Wisdom of the Fall

Do not be afraid to stumble,
to lose your footing
on the path you thought was yours.

The fall is not a failure,
but a redirection,
a chance to find a new way.

The ground that rushes up to meet you
is not an enemy,
but a teacher in disguise.

It whispers, "Look closer.
There are other paths
you were meant to explore."

Each bruise, each scrape,
is a lesson learned,
a reminder that growth
is not always linear.

Get up.
Dust yourself off.
The journey does not end here.
The wisdom you gain
is the compass that will guide you.

The Anatomy of Courage

Courage is not the absence of fear,
but the pulse that quickens
in the face of it.

It is the shaky hand
reaching for the unknown door,
the tremor in your voice
as you speak your truth.

It is the reason your heart
still beats, even when broken,
a rhythm of resilience
that will not be silenced.

Courage is not a roar,
but a whisper in the dark,
"I am still here.
I am still trying."

It is the way the body
holds both fear and hope
in the same breath,
a testament to the strength
that lies within your very being.

The Courage to Be Different

Do not be afraid to stand out,
to be different,
to walk a path that is uniquely yours.

The world does not need another fake.
It needs your originality,
your unique perspective,
your authentic voice.

It takes courage to be different,
to resist the pressure to conform,
to follow your own inner compass.

But in that courage,
there is a profound freedom,
a liberation from the expectations of others.

Embrace your quirks.
Celebrate your individuality.
The world needs your special kind of magic.

Dare to be different.
Dare to be you.
You are a masterpiece in the making.

The Courage to Begin Again

Every day is a new beginning,
a chance to start afresh,
to make different choices,
to create a new story.

Do not be bound by the past,
by your mistakes,
by your regrets.

You have the power to begin again,
no matter what has happened before.
It is never too late to change your path, to pursue your
dreams, to become the person you want to be.

Have the courage to begin again.
And again.
And again.

Each new beginning is an opportunity for growth,
for healing,
for transformation.

Embrace the possibilities that each new day brings.
Your future is unwritten.
Make it a good one.

The Strength in Vulnerability

Vulnerability is not weakness,
but a courageous act of strength.
It is daring to show up as you are,
without pretense,
without a mask,
without armor.

It is allowing yourself to be seen,
truly seen,
in all your imperfections,
in all your humanity.

Vulnerability is where connection is born,
where intimacy deepens,
where trust is built.

It is the pathway to authentic relationships,
both with others and with yourself.

Do not be afraid to be vulnerable.
Do not be afraid to let down your guard.
It takes courage, yes,
but the rewards are immeasurable.

In your vulnerability,
you will find your strength.
You will find your freedom.
You will find your true self.

Broken Heart

A heart that has never been broken
is a heart that has never fully lived.
It is in the breaking that the heart learns to expand,
to hold more love,
more compassion,
more empathy.

Discomfort is not the enemy of love,
but its teacher.
It shows you the depths of your capacity to feel,
to connect,
to be human.

A broken heart is not a tragedy.
It is an opportunity
to rebuild yourself stronger,
wiser,
more resilient than before.

The Strength of the Oak

The oak tree does not grow tall overnight.
It takes years,
decades,
centuries to reach its full height.

It weathers storms,
bends with the wind,
and its roots grow deeper,
its trunk grows stronger,
with each passing season.

Your strength is like the oak.
It does not grow rapidly,
but through the slow,
steady accumulation of resilience,
wisdom, and self-knowledge.

Embrace the gradual process of your growth.
Do not be discouraged by setbacks.
They are opportunities to deepen your roots,
to strengthen your resolve.

Slow growth is sustainable growth.
It is the foundation of a life that can weather any storm.

The Mountain and the Valley

The mountain does not lament the valley,
nor the valley the mountain.
Each has its purpose,
its unique beauty,
its essential role in the landscape.

Your challenges are not a sign of failure,
but an integral part of your journey,
like valleys shaping the grandeur
of your personal mountains.

From the valley, you learn resilience,
patience,
the strength to climb.

From the mountaintop, you gain perspective,
clarity,
a vision of how far you have come.

Embrace both the mountains and the valleys.
Shift your perspective to see not
a dichotomy of good and bad,
but a holistic picture of growth,
a landscape sculpted by experience,
leading you to higher peaks of understanding.

The Potter's Hands

Setbacks are not the end of your story,
but the potter's hands,
reshaping you,
refining you,
making you stronger.

You may feel you are being broken,
crushed under the weight of disappointment,
but you are being remade.

The potter knows the potential that lies within the clay.
The challenges you face are not meant to destroy you,
but to reveal your hidden strength,
your capacity for endurance,
your ability to rise from the ashes.

Trust the hands that are shaping you.
Embrace the process of being remade.
You are becoming something new,
something stronger,
something more beautiful than before.

The Breaking of the Mold

You were not born to fit a mold,
especially one that was cast generations ago.
You are a unique individual,
with your own gifts,
your own dreams,
your own path to walk.

It may feel uncomfortable to break the mold,
to step outside the familiar patterns.
There may be resistance,
both internal and external.

But you are not here to conform.
You are here to evolve.
You are here to become your truest self.

Breaking the mold is an act of courage,
an act of self-love,
an act of liberation.

It is saying "yes" to your own potential,
even when it means saying "no"
to the expectations of others.
It is choosing to live a life that is authentic,
even if it is different.

Do not be afraid to break the mold.
It is in the breaking that you find your freedom.
It is in the breaking that you find who you truly are.

Self-Love
and Acceptance

The Choice of Self-Love

Self-love is not a destination,
but a daily practice,
a quiet revolution
that begins within.

It is the choice to speak kindly
to the reflection in the mirror,
to forgive the mistakes of yesterday,
to honor the needs of your heart.

It is the act of nourishing your body,
not as punishment,
but as a temple of your soul.

It is setting boundaries
like protective walls around your spirit,
saying "no" to what harms you
and "yes" to what heals.

Self-love is not selfish,
it is survival.
It is the foundation upon which
a life of joy and purpose is built.

Choose yourself.
Again and again.
You are worthy of your love.

The Beauty of Imperfection

You are not flawed
because of the cracks that run through you.
They are the spaces
where the light gets in.

The scars you carry
are not symbols of defeat,
but reminders of your strength.

The parts of you that feel
broken, messy, unlovable,
are the very pieces
that make you whole.

You are not a mistake
to be fixed,
but a work in progress,
a mix of light and shadow,
perfect in your imperfection.

Embrace who you are.
You are the light
that shines through the broken places.
You are the strength
found in the dark.

The Wellspring of Enough

You do not need to earn your worthiness.
It is not a prize to be won,
a mountain to be climbed,
a destination to be reached.

It is a wellspring within you,
an ever-present source of love,
acceptance, and belonging.

You were born enough.
Whole.
Complete.

The world may have told you otherwise,
whispering doubts in your ear,
planting seeds of inadequacy.

But those are not your truths.
They are reflections of a world
that has forgotten its own inherent worth.

Turn away from the noise.
Turn inward.
Find the wellspring of enough within.

Drink deeply.
You are worthy.
You are deserving.
You are enough, just as you are.

The Masks We Wear

We learn to wear masks,
personas crafted to please,
to protect,
to hide the parts of ourselves
we were taught to deem unacceptable.

But behind the masks,
the true self yearns to breathe,
to be seen,
to be loved for who it truly is.

The masks may have served a purpose once,
shields in a world that felt unsafe.
But they become prisons
if we wear them for too long.

It takes courage to remove the masks,
to reveal the vulnerability beneath.

But in that unmasking,
there is liberation.
There is connection.
There is the possibility of being loved,
not for who you pretend to be,
but for the beautiful, imperfect soul you are.

The Gift of Letting Go

Letting go is not a defeat,
but a liberation,
a courageous act of surrender
to the flow of life.

It is releasing the grip
on what was,
on what could have been,
on who you thought you were supposed to be.

It is making space
for the new, the unknown,
the possibilities that await
when you open your heart.

Letting go is not easy.
It takes courage and faith.
But it is the key
to unlocking your true potential.

Release the past.
Release the pain.
Escape the expectations.

In the emptiness that remains,
you will find freedom.
You will find yourself.
You will find the gifts that only come with letting go.

You are Enough

You are enough, not when you achieve more.
You are enough, not when you are finally perfect.
You are enough, not when you please everyone.
You are enough, right here and now.
Breathe that in.

You are more than your doubts.
You are more than your fears.
You are more than your mistakes.

You are worthy of love.
You are worthy of belonging.
You are worthy, just as you are.

Stop striving to become someone else.
And simply be.

Because you, in your essence, are enough.

The Body's Wisdom

Your body speaks a language older than words,
a language of sensations,
of impulses,
of intuitive knowing.

It whispers through the tightness in your chest,
the flutter in your stomach,
the subtle shifts in your energy.

It tells you when something is wrong,
when something is right,
when you need to rest,
when you need to move.

Do not dismiss the wisdom of your body.
Do not try to silence its voice
with distractions or denial.

Learn to listen,
to trust,
to honor its messages.

Your body is not just a vessel for your mind.
It is a wise and compassionate guide,
leading you toward balance,
healing, and a deeper connection to yourself.

The Sanctuary Within

When the world feels too loud,
too harsh, too demanding,
remember there is a sanctuary
within you.

A quiet place where the soul
can rest and mend,
where the noise fades
and peace descends.

Close your eyes.
Breathe deeply.
Feel the stillness
at your center.

This is where you are safe.
This is where you are strong.
This is where you remember
who you are.

The world outside may rage,
but within you is an unshakable calm,
a wellspring of resilience
that will never run dry.

Return to this sanctuary
whenever you need.
It is always there,
waiting to embrace you.

The Necessity of Self-Care

Self-care is not a luxury,
but a necessity,
a practice of tending to your body,
mind, and spirit.

It is not an indulgence,
but an investment,
a way of ensuring you have the energy
to show up fully in your life.

Self-care is not one-size-fits-all.

It is a personal practice,
a unique blend of activities
that nourish and replenish you.

It may be a quiet walk in nature,
a warm bath,
a creative pursuit,
a moment of stillness.

Make time for self-care each day.
Make it a priority.
Make it non-negotiable.

Through self-care you reconnect
with your inner strength,
your wisdom,
your joy.

The Language of the Body

Your body is not a burden,
but a messenger,
speaking a language of wisdom
you are just beginning to understand.

The tension in your shoulders
is a plea for rest.
The ache in your heart
is a call for compassion.

The tears that well up
are a release of what no longer serves you,
a cleansing rain
that makes way for new growth.

Listen to the whispers of your body.
It is telling you what you need.
It is guiding you toward healing.
It is showing you the path
to your truest self.

The Gift of Your Own Company

Learn to enjoy your own company.
It is in the solitude, in the quiet moments with
yourself that true self-discovery occurs.
You are a fascinating being, full of depth,
complexity, and beauty.

Do not be afraid to spend time alone.
Do not see it as loneliness,
but as an opportunity to connect with your inner self,
to explore your thoughts and feelings,
to nurture your soul.

Take yourself on dates.
Read books that inspire you.
Write in your journal.
Pursue your hobbies.

The more you enjoy your own company, the more
you will attract fulfilling relationships with others.
You will approach them from a place of wholeness,
rather than neediness.

Cherish your solitude.
It is a gift, a chance to truly get to know the most
important person in your life: you.

The Home Within

You have searched for home in other people,
in other places,
but true home resides within you.

It is the quiet space where you feel safe,
accepted, and loved unconditionally.
It is the ground of your being,
the foundation upon which you stand.

You do not need to earn your place here.
You belong simply because you exist.

When you feel lost,
when you feel adrift,
return to the home within.

It is always there,
waiting to welcome you back,
to remind you that you are whole,
you are loved,
you are home.

The Universe Within

You are not just a drop in the ocean.
You are the entire ocean in a drop.
A universe of potential residing within.

Within you lies the same creative force that birthed stars.
Lie courage and resilience in the face of any storm.
Lies the capacity for boundless love and compassion.

Never forget the vastness that you carry within.
You are much more than you appear to be.
More capable than you believe yourself to be.
More powerful than you have ever imagined.

Embrace your inner universe.
Explore its depths.
Unleash its power.
The world is waiting for the unique gifts
that only you can offer.

Inner Harmony

Within you resides a chorus of voices,
each vying for attention,
each representing a different aspect of yourself.

There is the inner child,
yearning for love and safety.
The critic,
demanding perfection.
The dreamer,
reaching for the stars.

Do not try to silence these voices.
Instead, become the conductor of your inner orchestra.
Listen to each voice with compassion.
Understand its needs and fears.

Integration is not about choosing one voice over the others.
It is about harmonizing them,
allowing each to contribute its unique melody
to the symphony of your being.

The Permission to Rest

Rest is not a reward you earn,
but a necessity you require.
It is not laziness,
but an act of self-preservation.

Give yourself permission to pause,
to replenish,
to simply be.

The world will keep spinning
even if you stop for a moment.
Your worth is not tied
to your busyness.

Rest is where you heal,
where you integrate,
where you reconnect with yourself.

It is in the stillness
that you find clarity,
that you hear the whispers of your soul.

Do not wait until you are depleted
to give yourself the gift of rest.
Make it a priority.
Make it a practice.
Make it sacred.

Healing
and Growth

The Open Door

When one door closes, do not stand staring at it,
longing for what was.
Turn around.
There is always another door waiting to open.

It may be a door you never noticed before
It may lead to a path you never considered.
It may open to a future more beautiful than you ever
imagined.

Letting go of what was can be painful.
But it is necessary to create space for what can be.

Have faith that there are new opportunities waiting for you.
Have the courage to walk through the open door.

The universe is full of possibilities.
And sometimes, a closed door is the greatest gift of all.
It's a chance to find new opportunities, and to grow.

The Wisdom of the Wound

Do not shy away from your wounds.
They are not weaknesses to be hidden,
but portals to deeper understanding.

Each wound holds a lesson,
a hidden truth about yourself,
about life.

It is in the broken places
that empathy is born,
that compassion takes root.

It is through facing your pain
that you discover your strength,
your resilience.

Do not be afraid to explore your wounds.
Tend to them with kindness.
Listen to their wisdom.

They are not scars to be ashamed of,
but badges of courage,
reminders that you have lived,
you have learned,
you have grown.

The Freedom of Forgiveness

Forgiveness is not a gift you give to others,
but a freedom you claim for yourself.
It is releasing the chains of resentment
that bind you to the past.

It is not about condoning what was done,
but about choosing to no longer carry
the weight of anger and pain.
It doesn't mean forgetting,
it means you get to decide how it affects you.

Forgiveness is a radical act of self-love.
It is choosing peace over bitterness,
liberation over suffering.

Forgive yourself for the mistakes you have made.
Forgive others for the ways they have hurt you.

In forgiveness, you will find
a lightness of being,
a space for healing to begin,
a freedom to move forward
unburdened by the past.

The Journey of a Thousand Beginnings

Healing is not a linear path.
It is a spiral, a circle, a maze,
a journey of a thousand beginnings.

There will be days when you feel like you are starting over,
days when old wounds reopen,
days when you stumble and fall.

Do not be discouraged.
This is part of the process.
Each return to the beginning
is an opportunity to learn, to grow,
to deepen your understanding of yourself.

You are not failing.
You are growing,
evolving,
becoming more whole with each season.

Trust the journey.
Embrace the setbacks.
Every beginning, no matter how small,
is a step toward healing.

The Beauty of Beginnings

Every ending is a new beginning,
a chance to write a new story,
to choose a different path.

Do not be afraid to start over.
Do not be afraid to let go of what is no longer serving you.

There is a magic in beginnings,
a sense of hope and possibility,
a freshness that invigorates the soul.

Embrace the blank page.
Embrace the unknown.
You are the author of your life.
What story do you want to tell?

Every sunrise is an invitation
to begin again,
to step into the light
with courage and grace.

The Power of Small Steps

You do not need to climb mountains
to make progress.
Small steps are just as powerful,
just as significant.

Each act of self-care,
each moment of mindfulness,
each choice to be kind to yourself,
is a victory.

Do not underestimate
the power of consistency,
of showing up for yourself
day after day,
even when it feels hard.

The journey of healing
is not a sprint, but a marathon,
a slow, steady unfolding
of your potential.

Celebrate the small steps.
They are the building blocks
of a life transformed.
They are the proof
that you are moving forward,
even when it feels
like you are standing still.

The Becoming

You are not a finished product,
but a work in progress,
a constant state of becoming.
Embrace the uncertainty,
the fluidity of your being.

You are allowed to change,
to evolve,
to shed old skins
and emerge anew.

Do not be afraid to outgrow
the labels others have placed upon you,
the limitations you have placed upon yourself.

You are a universe of possibilities,
waiting to be explored.
You are a story still being written.

Trust the process of your becoming.
It is a beautiful, messy,
unfolding.

And the artist
is you.

The Gift of a Second Chance

Every breath is a second chance,
a new opportunity to choose differently,
to act with more kindness,
to love more deeply.

Do not dwell on past mistakes.
Do not be defined by your regrets.
Every moment is a chance to begin anew.

Forgive yourself.
Forgive others.
Release the weight of what was.

Embrace the gift of a second chance.
And a third.
And a fourth.

Life is constantly offering you opportunities for renewal,
for growth,
for redemption.

Take them.
Make the most of them.
You are worthy of a fresh start,
no matter how many times you need one.

The Seed of Hope

Even in the darkest of times,
never lose sight of the seed of hope
that resides within you.

It may seem small,
fragile,
insignificant.

But it holds the potential
for a brighter future,
for growth,
for renewal.

Nurture that seed.
Tend to it with care.
Protect it from the storms of doubt and despair.

Water it with self-compassion.
Feed it with positive thoughts.
Give it the sunlight of self-belief.

And one day,
you will see it sprout,
blossom,
and flourish into something beautiful,
something strong,
something that will sustain you
through any darkness.

Hope is always there, even when you cannot see it. Hold on and you will make it through. You are strong.

One Step at a Time

Every great journey begins with a single step.
And so does the journey of healing,
of growth,
of self-discovery.

Do not be discouraged by the length of the road ahead.
Do not be overwhelmed by the challenges you face.

Focus on the next step.
And then the next.
And then the next.

Each small act of courage,
each moment of self-compassion,
each choice to move forward,
is a step in the right direction.

Trust the process.
Celebrate your progress.
You are stronger than you think.

And you are not alone on this journey.
Keep walking.
Keep growing.
You will reach your destination, one step at a time.
You will become the person you want to be.

The Reframing Lens

Your perspective is a lens
through which you view the world.
It can distort or clarify,
dim or illuminate.

When faced with a challenge,
try changing the lens.
Reframe the situation.

Instead of "Why is this happening to me?"
ask, "What is this teaching me?"

Instead of "I can't do this,"
say, "How can I learn to do this?"

Instead of "This is a failure,"
consider, "This is a redirection."

The power of reframing
lies in its ability to shift your focus
from the problem to the solution,
from the obstacle to the opportunity,
from the perceived ending to the potential beginning.

The Wisdom of the Seasons

Nature teaches us that every season has its purpose.
Winter's barrenness is essential for spring's renewal.
Summer's intensity gives way to autumn's release.

Your challenges are not meant to last forever.
They are seasons of your life,
each with its own lessons,
its own unique beauty.

When your soul is in winter,
remember that spring will come.
Shift your perspective from one of despair
to one of anticipation.

See the challenges not as punishments,
but as periods of dormancy,
of inner growth,
preparing you for a new season of blossoming.
A chance to renew and to grow stronger.

The Winding Path

Personal growth is not a linear ascent,
but a spiral path,
winding upwards,
sometimes circling back,
but always progressing.

You may revisit old lessons,
face familiar challenges,
encounter echoes of the past.

Do not be discouraged.
This is not regression.
It is an opportunity to deepen your understanding,
to heal old wounds,
to integrate new wisdom.

Each loop of the spiral
takes you to a higher perspective,
a broader view,
a deeper level of self-awareness.

Trust the spiral path.
It may seem circuitous,
but it is leading you
toward greater wholeness,
greater wisdom,
greater freedom.

The Building Blocks of Change

Think of change not as a monumental leap,
but as a structure built brick by brick,
choice by choice,
day by day.

Each act of self-care,
each moment of mindfulness,
each decision to choose a healthier path,
is a brick in the foundation of your new life.

It may seem slow,
this process of building,
but with each brick laid,
the structure grows stronger,
more resilient,
more beautiful.

Do not be discouraged if you do not see immediate results.
Trust the process.
Keep laying the bricks.

The structure of your dreams
is taking shape,
one small step at a time.

The Map Etched in Scars

Your scars are not flaws,
but a roadmap of your journey,
a testament to your resilience,
a reminder of the battles you have fought and survived.

Each scar tells a story,
a story of pain,
yes,
but also a story of healing,
of growth,
of transformation.

Do not be ashamed of your scars.
They are proof that you have lived,
that you have loved,
that you have survived.

They are a guide,
etched onto your very being,
showing you where you have been
and pointing you toward where you are meant to go.

Your scars are not a burden, but a gift.
They are the map that leads you to your purpose. They
show you how strong you are, and remind you that
you can overcome anything.

The Gift of Change

Everything changes.
Everything flows.
Nothing stays the same.

This is the law of impermanence,
and it is a gift, not a curse.

Because things change,
pain does not last forever.
Difficult times will pass.
There is always the possibility of renewal.

Because things change,
you are not stuck in the past.
You can create a new future.
You can always begin again.

Embrace the flow of life.
Do not cling to what is fading.
Do not resist what is emerging.

In the reality of impermanence,
there is freedom,
there is growth,
there is the constant opportunity
to become something new.

The Beauty of What Remains

After the storm has passed,
after the tears have dried,
after the pain has subsided,
what remains?

You remain.
Stronger.
Wiser.
More resilient than before.

The essence of who you are
cannot be broken,
cannot be destroyed.

It may be hidden for a time,
buried beneath the rubble of hardship,
but it is always there,
waiting to be rediscovered.

Look for the beauty in what remains.
The strength that has been forged in the fire.
The wisdom that has been gleaned from the ashes.

You are still here.
You are still whole.
And you are more beautiful than ever before. What
is left after the storm is the strongest part of you.

Connection
and Belonging

Love's Awakening

Love begins as a spark,
a flicker of recognition,
a feeling of warmth that spreads through your being.

It is an awakening,
a quickening of the heart,
a sense of coming alive in the presence of another.

It may be a sudden, unexpected blaze,
or a slow, gentle ember that grows over time.

But when love awakens,
the world is transformed.

Colors seem brighter,
music sounds sweeter,
and the ordinary becomes extraordinary.

It is a feeling of expansion,
of connection,
of being seen and known and cherished
for who you truly are.

The awakening of love is a powerful emotion,
a profound experience,
a reminder of the beauty and joy
that life has to offer.

The Mirror of Love

Love is a mirror,
reflecting back to you the beauty,
the goodness,
the light that resides within.

When you are truly seen and loved by another,
you begin to see yourself through their eyes.
You begin to recognize your own worth,
your own lovability.

The love of another can awaken you
to the love that already exists within you.
It can remind you of your own capacity for compassion,
for kindness,
for connection.

Love is a powerful teacher,
a guide that leads you back to yourself,
to the heart of who you truly are.

The Roots and the Branches

The roots of family run deep,
anchoring you to a lineage,
a history that stretches back through time.

But you are not just the roots.
You are also the branches,
reaching toward the sunlight,
growing in your own direction.

You can honor the roots,
acknowledge the lessons they hold,
without being confined by them.

You can draw strength from your heritage
while choosing which parts to carry forward,
and which to leave behind.

It is not a betrayal to grow beyond the limitations
of your ancestors.
It is an act of evolution,
a testament to the resilience of the human spirit.

You are the bridge between the past and the future.
Choose to build a future that is free,
expansive, and truly your own.

Belonging

You are not a solitary thread,
but a vital part of something larger,
a community of souls,
interwoven and interconnected.

You belong here.
You are needed.
Your presence makes a difference.

Do not isolate yourself in pain,
in doubt,
in fear.

Reach out.
Connect.
Share your story.
You will find that you are not alone.

There are others who understand,
who have walked a similar path,
who can offer support and companionship.

We are all connected,
all part of the same human family.

In that belonging,
there is strength,
there is healing,
there is hope.

Our Shared Humanity

Beyond the circles of our personal relationships
lies the possibility of an expansive love for all of humanity,
a recognition of our interconnectedness,
a compassion that can extend to strangers,
a desire for the well-being of all beings.

Though often challenged by the realities of the world,
It is the understanding that we are all part
of the same human family,
sharing the same planet,
facing the same fundamental challenges,
yearning for the same basic needs of love,
belonging, and meaning.

This love for humanity calls us to act with kindness,
to work toward justice,
to build bridges of understanding across divides.
It is a call we must strive to answer.

It is a love that has the power to heal the world,
one act of compassion at a time.
It is a love worth fighting for.
It is a love that starts with seeing the humanity
and the light in others.

The World Awaits Your Gift

You are not meant to keep your gifts hidden away.
The world is waiting for what you have to offer.
It needs your unique perspective, your talents,
and your light.

Do not let fear hold you back.
Do not let self-doubt silence your voice.
Do not let the opinions of others define your path.

Step into your power.
Embrace your gifts.
Share them with the world.

Your contribution may seem small to you,
but it can make a profound difference to others.
It can be the spark that ignites a fire.
The seed that blossoms into something beautiful.

The world is waiting for you.
Waiting for your unique magic.
Waiting for the gifts that only you can bring.

It is time to answer the call and share your gifts
with those who need them.

The Roots of Empathy

Empathy is not a passive feeling,
but a bridge that connects us,
heart to heart,
soul to soul.
It is the ability to see yourself in another,
to recognize that their struggles are your struggles,
their joys are your joys,
their humanity is your humanity.

Empathy grows from the roots of self-awareness.
When you understand your own pain,
you can understand the pain of others.
When you have known suffering,
you can offer compassion.

Empathy is the foundation of social equity.
It compels you to act,
to speak out against unfairness,
to work toward a world where everyone has the
opportunity to thrive.

Tend to the roots of empathy within you.
This is the path to deeper self-understanding
and a more profound connection to all of humanity.
Let empathy guide you to build bridges, not walls.

The Fabric of We

Your story is not a solo performance.
It is interwoven with the stories of countless others,
a fabric of shared experiences,
struggles, and triumphs.

Your well-being is ultimately your own responsibility.
But it is nurtured and strengthened
by a collective endeavor,
a shared commitment to creating a world
where everyone can thrive.

We rise by lifting others.
We heal by helping others heal.
We find our own liberation
in working toward the liberation of all.

Embrace the "we" in your journey of personal growth.
Recognize that your individual well-being
is inextricably linked to the well-being
of the larger community.

Together, we can weave a fabric of justice,
equality, and shared prosperity.

The Lighthouse Effect

When you find true connection,
you become a lighthouse for others,
and they for you,
guiding each other through the storms of life
with the unwavering light of connection.

You shine a light on their strengths,
reminding them of their worth
when they have forgotten.

They, in turn, illuminate your path,
offering guidance,
wisdom, and a safe harbor
when you feel lost at sea.

Together, you create a web of support,
a network of beacons
that pierce through the darkness,
reminding you that even in the midst of uncertainty,
you are never truly alone.

These connections will help you navigate life.
And you will do the same for them.
Together, you will make it through any storm.

The Mirror of the Soul

Every person you meet is a mirror,
reflecting back to you aspects of your own soul.
The qualities you admire in others
are qualities that reside within you.

While some judgments arise from genuine differences,
often the qualities we judge most harshly in others
are those we have not yet accepted in ourselves.
The love you give to others
is a reflection of the love you hold within.

Every interaction is an opportunity for self-discovery.
Look into the mirror of the soul.
What do you see?
What can you learn about yourself from
your interactions with others?

We are all teachers and students on this path.
We learn from each other.
We grow through our connections.

The outer world is a reflection of your inner world.
Pay attention to the mirrors around you.
They hold the keys to your own transformation.

The Web of Being

You are not a solitary island,
but a thread in the vast web of being,
intricately connected to all things.

The air you breathe
is the same air that rustles the leaves,
that fills the sails of ships,
that whispers through the canyons.

The water within you
is the same water that carves mountains,
that nourishes the forests,
that fills the vast, deep ocean.

The fire in your heart
is the same fire that fuels the sun,
that sparks innovation,
that ignites the spirit of life.

You are made of stardust,
of earth and water and air,
a microcosm of the universe,
reflecting the macrocosm outside.

Your joys and sorrows ripple outwards,
touching the lives of others,
just as their experiences touch you.

We are all connected,
human, nature, and the cosmos,
a symphony of being,
playing out in the grand theater of existence.

The River of Connection

We are all flowing down the same river of life,
connected by the current of existence.
Sometimes the waters are calm and peaceful,
sometimes they are turbulent and challenging.

But we are not alone in our journey.
The joys and sorrows of others
flow alongside our own.
Their struggles and triumphs mirror ours.

When you reach out a hand to someone in need,
you are also reaching into the depths of your own being.
When you offer compassion to another,
you are also offering it to yourself.

We are all connected by this shared journey,
this river of life that flows through us all.
Recognize this connection.
Embrace it.

In our interconnectedness,
we find strength,
we find solace,
we find our way back to ourselves.

Beyond Borders, One Heart

Beyond the lines drawn on maps,
beyond the flags that wave in the wind,
beyond the anthems sung in different tongues,
beats a single, shared human heart.

We may speak diverse languages,
hold varied beliefs,
walk different paths under different skies,
but our deepest desires are the same.

To live in peace,
to see our children thrive,
to build a world where hope outweighs fear,
where understanding bridges ancient divides.

Let us choose to see beyond the borders,
to recognize the light of shared humanity
that shines in every soul,
in every corner of this earth.

Let us lay down the weapons of prejudice and distrust,
and build bridges of dialogue and respect,
paving the way for a future
where cooperation triumphs over conflict,
where peace is not a distant dream,
but a shared reality we create, together.

The world we strive for is within our reach.
It begins with a simple choice.
To see each other not as strangers or as enemies,
but as fellow travelers on this precious planet,
bound by a common destiny,
united by a single, shared human heart.
Let us choose to work together to create
the world we want to live in.

The Legacy We Leave Behind

We are not just individuals,
but links in a chain that stretches
across generations.

The choices we make today,
the actions we take,
the way we treat one another,
will shape the legacy we leave behind.

Will we pass on the wounds of the past,
or will we choose to create a future
defined by healing,
by justice,
by love?

The power to shape that legacy lies within each of us.
Let us choose to be healers,
bridge-builders,
weavers of a brighter future.

Let us create a world where our children
and our children's children
can thrive,
free from the burdens of the past,
empowered to create a more beautiful tomorrow.
Our choices today affect the world of tomorrow.

Nature's
Lessons

The River's Wisdom

The river does not rage
against the rocks that impede its flow.
It does not lament the bends and curves,
the unexpected turns, the sudden falls.
It simply moves, adapts, persists.

Your life too, is a current.
There will be obstacles,
moments that feel like setbacks,
times when you are forced to change course.
Do not fight the flow.

Learn from the river.
Adjust your path,
change your course.
Embrace the detours.
Know that even in the stillness,
you are moving, you are growing.
The journey is not about perfection,
but about the unwavering current
of your spirit, flowing ever onward,
carving its own unique path
to the vast and boundless sea.

The Mirror's Truth

The mirror does not lie,
But, it only shows you a surface.
It reflects the shape of your body,
the lines on your face,
but it cannot capture the light in your soul,
the depth of your compassion,
the strength of your spirit.

Stop searching for validation
in the reflection.
The world will try to define you
by fleeting standards,
by ever-shifting expectations.
But true beauty is not a picture, not a visual, nor an image;
it is a radiance that emanates from within.

Choose to see yourself
with the eyes of your heart.
Acknowledge the battles you've fought,
the kindness you've shown,
the love you hold within.
You are not just a reflection,
you are a universe,
a constellation of stardust and dreams.
You are worth far more than gold.
Love every inch of the masterpiece you are.

The Emotional Ocean

Your emotions are like the ocean,
vast, deep, and ever-changing.
Do not be afraid to dive into their depths.

There will be calm, peaceful waters,
and there will be stormy, turbulent waves.
There will be moments of joy and moments of sorrow.

It is all part of the human experience.
It is all welcome.
It all teaches you something about yourself.

Do not try to suppress your emotions
or numb yourself to their intensity.
Allow yourself to feel them fully,
without judgment,
without resistance.

In the depths of your emotional ocean,
you will find treasures of wisdom,
compassion, and self-understanding.

Accept the changing tides of your emotions.
They are what make you human.
They are your connection to life.

The Wisdom of the Trees

Learn from the wisdom of the trees.
They stand tall and grounded,
their roots reaching deep into the earth,
their branches reaching toward the sky.

They bend with the wind,
but they do not break.
They weather the storms,
knowing that they will pass.

They let go of their leaves in the autumn,
trusting that new growth will come in the spring.
They are patient.
They are resilient.

They are connected to the earth,
to the seasons,
to the cycle of life and death.

Like the trees,
you too are grounded in something deeper than yourself.
You too can bend without breaking.
You too can weather any storm.

Remember the wisdom of the trees.
Stand tall.
Stay grounded.
Trust the cycles of your life.

The Breath of the Universe

The universe breathes,
and so do you.
A constant cycle of expansion and contraction,
of giving and receiving,
of life and death.

You are not separate from this cosmic breath.
You are an integral part of it.
Every inhale is a gift from the universe.
Every exhale is a release back into the whole.

When you feel lost or disconnected,
remember the breath.
It is your connection to all things,
a reminder that you are part of something
larger than yourself.

The universe breathes through you.
Feel its rhythm.
Trust its flow.

You are a vital part of this grand cosmic dance,
connected to every star,
every galaxy,
every atom in existence.

The Unity of Opposites

Life is a dance of opposites,
yin and yang,
light and dark,
creation and destruction.

These forces are not in conflict,
but in a dynamic interplay,
each containing the seed of the other,
each essential to the whole.

Embrace the duality of existence.
Seek balance, not by eliminating one side,
but by harmonizing both.

Find the stillness in motion,
the light in the darkness,
the strength in vulnerability.

In the unity of opposites lies the key to wholeness,
to a life that is both dynamic and peaceful,
grounded and transcendent.

Facing the Unknown

The future is a mystery,
a vast expanse of unknown possibilities.
Do not fear it.
Embrace it.

You do not need to have all the answers.
You do not need to know exactly where you are going.
Trust that the path will unfold before you,
one step at a time.

Be open to surprises,
to detours,
to unexpected opportunities.

The unknown is not something to be feared,
but something to be explored,
with curiosity,
with wonder,
with an open heart.

In facing the unknown,
you will discover new strengths,
hidden talents,
and a deeper understanding of yourself
and the world around you.

Inner Seasons

Just as the earth has its seasons,
so too does the inner self.

There are times for growth and blossoming,
times for harvest and abundance,
times for rest and introspection,
and times for letting go and renewal.

Each season has its purpose,
its own unique beauty,
its own set of lessons.

Do not try to force yourself to be in perpetual summer.

Embrace the natural rhythm of your inner seasons.

Honor the need for rest and retreat,
just as you celebrate the times of expansion and joy.

In the cyclical nature of these inner seasons,
you will find a deeper understanding of yourself,
a greater appreciation for the fullness of life,
and a profound connection to the natural world.

The River's Path

The river does not rush to the sea.
It meanders,
it flows,
it follows the contours of the land.

It understands that the journey
is as important as the destination,
that every twist and turn
shapes its course.

Your path to healing
will not be linear.
There will be curves,
and bends,
and unexpected detours.

Do not resist the flow.
Do not try to force a shortcut.
Trust that the river of your life
is leading you where you need to go.

Embrace the slow,
organic process of your journey.
The beauty lies in the unfolding.

The River of Time

Life is a river,
constantly flowing,
ever-changing,
never the same.

Time carries you along its current,
sometimes slowly,
sometimes swiftly,
through calm waters and turbulent rapids.

You cannot stop the river's flow,
nor can you turn back the hands of time.
But you can choose how you navigate the waters.

You can resist the current,
struggling against the flow,
or you can surrender to its movement,
trusting that it will carry you where you need to go.

Embrace the river of time.
Appreciate each moment as it passes.
Learn from the past,
but don't look back, you're not going that way.
Look to the future,
but do not lose yourself in it.

Be fully present in the flow of your life,
and you will find peace,
purpose, and a deep appreciation for the journey.

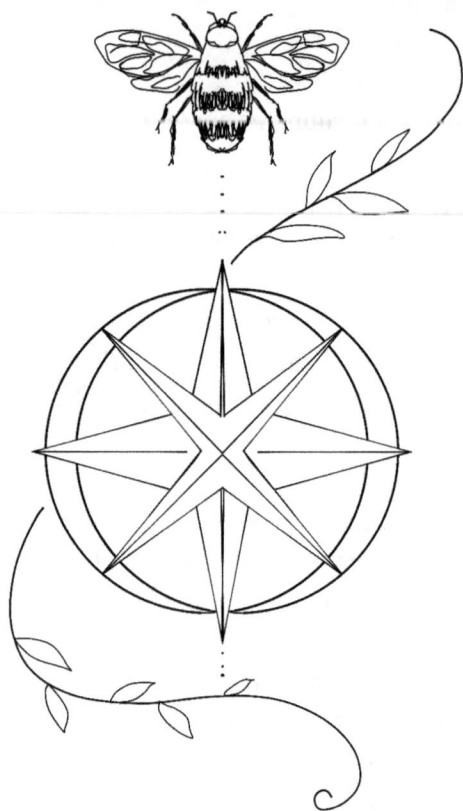

Purpose
and Authenticity

The Unfolding of Your Purpose

Your purpose is not a destination to be reached,
but a path to be walked,
a continuous unfolding
of your unique gifts.

It is not something you find,
but something you create,
moment by moment,
choice by choice.

It is not a grand, singular act,
but a series of small offerings,
ways of showing up in the world
that align with your values.

Your purpose may shift and evolve
over time,
and that is okay.
You are not meant to be static.

Trust the journey.
Trust the process.
Your purpose is not a burden,
but a joy,
a way of sharing your light
with the world.

Choose Your Own Metric

They measure success in numbers,
in dollars and cents,
in square footage and followers,
in titles and trophies.

But you are not a number.
You are not a commodity.
You are a human being,
with a soul that yearns for something more.

Have the courage to choose your own metric.
Measure your success in moments of joy,
in acts of kindness,
in the depth of your connections,
in the impact you make on the world.

Measure it in the way you feel when
you wake up in the morning.
And how you feel when you go to bed at night.
Measure it in the love you give and receive.

Success is not a competition.
It is a personal truth.
And you are the only one who can know it.
You hold the key to what true success is for you.

The Edge of the Comfort Zone

The comfort zone is a cozy nest,
a place of familiar warmth and safety.
But growth does not happen in comfort.

It happens at the edge,
where the known meets the unknown,
where you are challenged to stretch,
to expand,
to become more than you were before.

Stepping beyond the familiar, sparks discomfort,
a clear sign you are on the path of growth,
an invitation to explore new terrain,
to discover hidden strengths.

Do not be afraid to venture to the edge.
That is where you will find your wings,
where you will learn to fly,
where you will discover what you are truly capable of.

The Scroll and the Soul

The screen glows, a siren's call,
promising connection, yet holding us captive
in a world of curated selves and filtered realities.

We scroll through endless feeds,
seeking validation in likes and hearts,
yet feeling a deeper disconnect within.

The digital age has woven itself into our lives,
but has it woven its way into our souls?

Do not lose yourself in the curated perfection.
Remember the messy, imperfect, beautiful
truth of who you are.
The soul needs more than a curated reality,
it needs authenticity.

Unplug.
Look up.
The real world, with all its imperfections, awaits.
Your heart, not the internet, holds the truest connection.
Your soul can't be found on a screen,
but in lived experience.

The Cage of Expectations

Expectations, both our own and others', can become a cage,
confining us to narrow definitions of success,
happiness, and worth.

These bars are often invisible,
but they are strong.
They limit our choices,
stifle our dreams,
and keep us from exploring
the fullness of who we are.

Question the expectations that bind you.
Are they truly yours?
Or are they echoes of voices
you have internalized,
societal pressures you have absorbed?

The key to unlocking the cage
is to redefine your own values,
to listen to the whispers of your own heart,
to forge your own path,
even if it deviates from the well-trodden road.

The Blueprint of Belonging

We are taught to seek belonging
by conforming, by fitting in, by molding ourselves to
external standards.
But true belonging is not found in sameness, but in
authenticity.

It is about finding your tribe,
the people who see you,
who hear you,
who love you for who you truly are,
not for who they want you to be.

The blueprint of belonging
is not written in the rules of society,
but in the language of your heart.

It requires you to be brave enough to show up as yourself,
to speak your truth,
to embrace your quirks,
to celebrate your uniqueness.

When you find the courage to belong to yourself first,
you will discover that true belonging
is not about fitting in,
but about standing out,
in all your radiant, authentic glory. You will find people
who love you for who you are, not despite it.

The Power of One Transformed Life

Never doubt the power of one transformed life.
Yours.
It is a catalyst for change,
a ripple that can become a wave.

When you choose to heal,
to grow,
to embrace your authentic self,
you inspire others to do the same.

Your journey becomes a testament
to the resilience of the human spirit,
a beacon of hope for those
who are still struggling.

One transformed life can touch countless others,
creating a ripple effect of positive change
that extends far beyond
what you can see or imagine.

Trust in the power of your journey.
Trust in the ripple effect.
You are changing the world,
one step, one breath, one act of courage at a time.

The Crossroads Within

You stand at a crossroads within your heart,
one path paved with fear, the other with love.
One whispers doubts, the other breathes hope.
The choice is yours, in every moment.

Fear is a shadow, a constricting force,
that feeds on insecurity and thrives in darkness.
It builds walls of protection that become prisons,
isolating you from the very connection you crave.

Love is a light, an expansive force,
that illuminates your path and warms your soul.
It tears down walls and builds bridges,
connecting you to yourself, to others, to the world.

Choose love.
It may not always be the easier path.
It requires courage to be vulnerable,
to open your heart when it has been wounded.

But love is the path to freedom,
to growth, to a life lived fully.
Choose love, and watch your world transform.

The Mirror of the Moment

Every interaction is a mirror,
reflecting back not just the other,
but also yourself.

Do you react with defensiveness,
with anger,
with a need to be right?
Or do you respond with empathy,
with understanding,
with a willingness to learn?

The mirror shows you where you are still triggered,
where you are still holding onto old wounds.
It also reveals your capacity for growth, for compassion,
for conscious engagement.

Look closely.
What do you see?
And more importantly, what will you choose
to do with what you see?

The choice is always yours.
Choose to respond, not react.
Choose to learn from the reflection.

The Inner Ecosystem

Within you lies an ecosystem,
as complex and diverse as any on earth.
Thoughts, emotions, beliefs, and sensations,
intertwined and interdependent.

Your inner landscape mirrors the outer world.
The storms that rage within
reflect the storms that rage without.
The peace you cultivate inside
ripples outwards into your life.

When you neglect one aspect of your being,
the entire system is affected.
Unprocessed emotions fester like stagnant pools.
Negative thoughts cloud the inner sky.

But when you tend to your inner garden,
when you cultivate self-awareness,
compassion, and acceptance,
you create a thriving ecosystem within.

You are not separate from your inner world.
It is the foundation upon which your outer world is built.
Heal the inner, and you heal the outer.
They are reflections of each other, always.

Listen Within

Listen closely.
Can you hear it?

The music within you,
a melody that is uniquely yours.

It may be a quiet whisper,
a subtle rhythm,
a powerful anthem.

It is the song of your heart,
your passions,
your dreams,
your deepest desires.

Do not let the noise of the world
drown out this inner music.

Make time to listen,
to appreciate the melody within.

Let it guide you,
inspire you,
lead you to a life that is authentic,
meaningful, and true to who you are.

Move to your own rhythm.

Sing your own song.

The world is waiting to hear it.

The Architect of Your Thoughts

You are the architect of your thoughts,
the master builder of your inner reality.
Choose your materials wisely.

Will you build with bricks of fear and doubt,
or with stones of courage and self-belief?
Will you construct walls that confine you,
or bridges that connect you to new possibilities?

Your thoughts are the blueprints of your life.
They shape your perceptions,
influence your emotions,
and determine your actions.

Take responsibility for your mental architecture.
Demolish the structures that no longer serve you.
Design a life that is aligned with your values,
your dreams,
your highest potential.

You have the power to rebuild,
to renovate,
to create a mental dwelling
that is filled with light,
with peace,
with unwavering strength.

The Inner Compass

When life throws you off course,
and you find yourself lost in a sea of doubt,
remember the inner compass that resides within you.

It is your intuition,
your inner wisdom,
your connection to your true self.

It may be a quiet voice,
a subtle feeling,
a gentle nudge in a certain direction.

Learn to trust that inner compass.
It knows the way,
even when your mind is clouded by fear or confusion.

Resilience is not just about outer strength,
but about inner guidance,
about listening to the wisdom that lies within you,
and having the courage to follow where it leads.

The Unmasking

Deconstructing the ego
is not a battle to be won,
but a gentle unraveling,
a process of unmasking.

It is recognizing the ego's games,
its need for control,
its fear of the unknown.

It is seeing through the illusions
it has created,
the stories it has spun,
the limitations it has imposed.

Unmasking is not about destroying the ego,
but understanding its role,
and choosing to no longer be ruled by it.
It is seeing that the ego is part of you, but
it is not the whole of who you are.

It is a journey of liberation,
a return to your true self,
a self that is boundless,
free, and inherently whole.

Saying No

"No" is not a negative word,
but a powerful affirmation of your priorities,
a declaration of self-respect,
a protection of your precious energy.

It is a complete sentence.
It does not require justification or apology.
It is a boundary that creates space for what truly matters.

Do not be afraid to say "no"
to requests that drain you,
to commitments that overwhelm you,
to relationships that deplete you.

Each "no" you utter creates space for a "yes"
to something that aligns with your values,
to something that nourishes your soul,
to something that honors your energy.

Saying "no" is an act of self-love.
It is a way of choosing yourself,
of honoring your limits,
of creating a life that is truly your own.

The Illusion of the Finish Line

They told you success was a finish line,
a destination to be reached,
a prize to be won.

But what if success is not a place,
but a way of being,
a way of moving through the world,
a way of living in alignment
with your deepest self?

What if it's not about the accolades,
the achievements,
the external markers of validation,
but about the internal landscape
of peace,
joy, and fulfillment?

Release the need to chase a phantom finish line.
Embrace the journey.
Find success in the everyday moments,
in the choices you make,
in the way you treat yourself and others.

Success is not a destination.
It is a way of life, lived on your own terms.

The Fusion of Loving What You Do

Great work is not born from obligation,
but from the fusion of passion and purpose combined.
It is the result of loving what you do,
a love that transforms the ordinary into the meaningful.

When you love your work,
it ceases to be mere labor,
and becomes an act of creation,
an offering to the world,
a reflection of your deepest self.

This love is not always easy to find.
It requires courage,
introspection,
and a willingness to break free from the mold.

But when you find it,
you will know.
It will feel like coming home,
like finally breathing after being held underwater.
It will heal the parts of you that felt fractured
and incomplete.

The Mirror of Justice

Social justice is not just a cause to be fought for "out there."
It is a mirror reflecting the work we must do within.

The biases we hold.
The privileges we carry.
The ways we have internalized oppression.

To create a more just world,
we must first examine our own hearts.
We must dismantle the systems of injustice
that reside within our own minds.

Your personal growth is a journey of unlearning,
of confronting your own shadows,
of transforming your inner landscape.

As you cultivate empathy and understanding within,
you become a more powerful agent of change in the world.
Justice begins with the self, and radiates outwards.

Author's Note

Welcome to Soul Honey, a collection of poems about self-love, healing, and self-discovery. These poems explore the journey inward, the power of embracing our imperfections, and the strength we find in mending our own hearts.

The title, Soul Honey, reflects the nourishing sweetness that comes from turning inward with compassion. It's a reminder that we can create a rich, meaningful life by embracing all our experiences, both the bitter and the sweet.

My hope is that these poems will feel like a comforting hand on your journey, offering solace and a gentle nudge toward your inner light. I hope they remind you that you're worthy of love, especially your own, and that healing is a path of continuous growth.

This book is for all of us, all of us who are trying our best. It is to show that we are all connected, and as we grow as individuals, we make the world better.

May these poems offer you comfort and inspiration.

With love,
Michael Mosesian

Acknowledgments:

Like the honey that inspired this book's title, this collection was created through a process of gathering, refining, and transforming. And just as bees work together in a hive, this book is the result of many hearts and hands.

To my family and friends, you are my hive, my source of unwavering support. Your love has been the foundation upon which I could build, heal, and grow.

To those who offered early feedback on these poems, your insights were like flowers, each one unique and essential to the creation of this honey.

Thank you to Melanie for your insightful feedback and guidance, which helped shape this collection into its final form.

A special thank you to Katrina for designing the beautiful cover illustration that sets the tone for these pages, and to Fatima for creating the illustrations for each chapter. Your work truly enhances this collection.

To my readers, may these poems nourish your soul and remind you of the beauty within and around you. Thank you for being part of this journey.

Finally, if you enjoyed Soul Honey, I'd love to connect with you on social media! I share new poems and reflections there regularly. Every new follower, every like, every share truly makes my day.

Instagram: @mosesianpoetry
TikTok: @mosesianpoetry